Exploring Asian Cultures Through Crafts

Mia Farrell

Enslow Publishing
101 W. 23rd Street
Suite 240
New York, NY 10011
USA

enslow.com

Published in 2016 by Enslow Publishing, LLC.
101 W. 23rd Street, Suite 240, New York, NY 10011

Cataloging-in-Publication Data
Farrell, Mia.
Exploring Asian cultures through crafts / by Mia Farrell.
p. cm. — (Multicultural crafts)
Includes bibliographical references and index.
ISBN 978-0-7660-6774-5 (library binding)
ISBN 978-0-7660-6773-8 (pbk.)
ISBN 978-0-7660-6776-9 (6-pack)
1. Handicraft — Asia — Juvenile literature. 2. Handicraft — Juvenile literature. I. Title.
TT160.F377 2016
745.5095—d23

Printed in the United States of America

To Our Readers: We have done our best to make sure all Web site addresses in this book were active and appropriate when we went to press. However, the author and the publisher have no control over and assume no liability for the material available on those Web sites or on any Web sites they may link to. Any comments or suggestions can be sent by e-mail to customerservice@enslow.com.

Portions of this book originally appeared in the book *Asian-American Crafts Kids Can Do!* by Sarah Hartman.

Photo Credits: Crafts prepared by June Ponte; craft photography by Lindsay Pries. Andra Simionescu/Digital Vision Vectors/Getty Images (background throughout book); © AP Images, p. 6; Barry Chin/The Boston Globe via Getty Images, p. 22; Barry Kusuma/Photolibrary/Getty Images, p. 16; blue jean images/Getty Images, p. 14; DEA / G. CIGOLINI/De Agostini Picture Library/Getty Images, p. 8; Godong/Universal Images Group/Getty Images, p. 18; John S Lander/LightRocket/Getty Images, p. 5; Keren Su/Stone/Getty Images, p. 24; mileswork/Shutterstock.com, p. 1 (Earth icon); Multi-bits/Photolibrary/Getty Images, p. 12; Oliver Strewe/Lonely Planet Images/Getty Images, p. 4; Otto Stadler/Photographer's Choice RF/Getty Images, p. 10; Tosa Mitsunobu/Wikimedia Commons/Kiyomizudera engi emaki - Scroll1 Pic8.jpg/public domain, p. 20.

Cover Credits: Crafts prepared by June Ponte; craft photography by Lindsay Pries. Andra Simionescu/Digital Vision Vectors/Getty Images (background); mileswork/Shutterstock.com (Earth icon).

CONTENTS

Asian Cultures and Crafts 4

Kamishibai 6

Japanese Paper Fan 8

Shadow Puppet From Bali 10

Picture Frame With Korean
Ornamental Knots 12

Paper Cutting From China 14

Theater Mask From Indonesia 16

Tibetan Sand Mandala 18

Emaki Story Scroll 20

Origami Jumping Frog 22

Paper Non From Vietnam 24

Patterns 26

Learn More 30

Web Sites 31

Index 32

Safety Note: *Be sure to ask for help from an adult, if needed, to complete these crafts!*

ASIAN CULTURES AND CRAFTS

Asian customs come from many countries, regions, and traditions. The culture of Indonesia is very different from that of China. But these customs have many similarities, as well.

Over the centuries, the crafts and their styles have changed. Other people and their traditions mixed with these crafts. For

Paper lanterns are a Chinese tradition.

Zen gardens are common in Japan.

example, people who make scrapbooks often use paper cutting to decorate the pages. Paper cutting is a Chinese art form.

Asian crafts are known throughout the world: from silk to fans to masks, these crafts can be found in stores today. But some of these things can be made at home, with common household items. Zen gardens can be made from shoeboxes. Lanterns can be made from construction paper. Learn to make your own Asian crafts.

KAMISHIBAI

Before the days of television, storytelling was a common form of entertainment. Japanese storytellers went from town to town on bicycles, setting up a wooden theater-shaped box called a kamishibai (kah-mee-she-bye). These entertainers would illustrate their stories with pictures placed in the kamishibai.

A storyteller performs kamishibai for a group of children in Japan.

WHAT YOU WILL NEED

- shoebox
- scissors
- construction paper
- crayons or markers
- glue
- large index cards

1. With the shoebox on its side, cut a slot in the top side of your box, all the way from one side to the other.

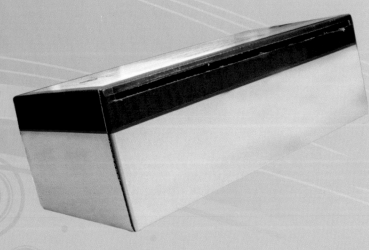

2. Cover the outside of the box in construction paper. Do not cover the slot. Decorate the outside of the box with crayons, markers, or different colors of paper. Put the box back on its side with the slotted side up.

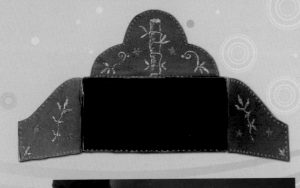

3. Choose a story or make one up. On the index cards, draw pictures that show the things happening in the story. Stack the cards in the order the pictures should appear in the story.

4. Drop the first picture into the slot and begin telling the story. Drop pictures into the slot as they come up in the story. The pictures should fall in front of each other so the audience sees each new picture.

JAPANESE PAPER FAN

This fan shows a scene from family life.

Before the invention of air conditioning, fans helped keep people cool during the summer. Part of Japanese culture, traditional Japanese fans made living with nature easier. Today, these fans are also used for decoration.

WHAT YOU WILL NEED

- poster board or paper plate
- scissors
- 3 craft sticks
- markers
- glue

1. Cut a large circle out of poster board, or just use a paper plate.

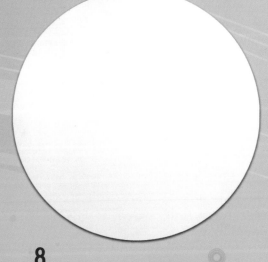

2. Decorate the paper circle however you'd like. Write a story or poem. Sketch a drawing or shapes. Use whatever colors you want to.

3. Glue the craft sticks together in a Y shape, and then glue the sticks to the back of the fan. The Y shape is the handle of the fan.

4. After your fan is dry, it is ready to keep you cool or decorate your wall.

SHADOW PUPPET FROM BALI

In Bali, shadow plays are a favorite way to tell stories. Storytellers use shadow plays to tell stories about history, religion, as well as funny, sad, or scary stories. Some shadow plays are performed by one person who works up to twenty puppets.

Shadow puppets help tell a story.

WHAT YOU WILL NEED

- poster board
- scissors
- pencil
- hole punch
- ½-inch (1¼-centimeter) brass fasteners
- clear tape
- 4 nonbendable drinking straws

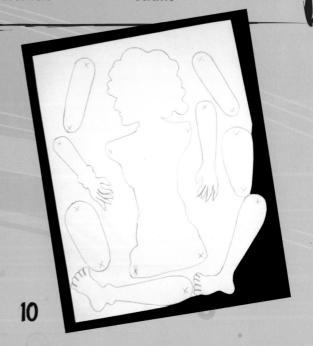

1. Using the pattern on page 29, trace the Balinese shadow puppet patterns onto poster board. Cut out 4 arm pieces, 2 top leg pieces, 2 bottom leg pieces, and 1 body piece.

10

2. Punch holes in all the pieces where an X is marked on the pattern. Use brass fasteners to connect the leg pieces together, the arm pieces together, and the arms and legs to the body.

3. Decorate the puppet.

4. Tape straws to the ends of the puppet's legs and arms. Use these straws to hold the puppet up and make it dance or act out a story.

PICTURE FRAME WITH KOREAN ORNAMENTAL KNOTS

The art of knot tying has been taught in Korea for centuries. These knots were used to decorate furniture, clothes, and mirrors. There were special knots for brides and religious ceremonies, as well as knots for bags, spoons, chopsticks, hats, and other common items.

In Korean tradition, many gifts are wrapped by knotting cloth or paper.

WHAT YOU WILL NEED

- pencil
- colored paper
- 2 large index cards
- scissors
- glue

1. Using the pattern on page 26, trace the knot pattern onto paper. Cut an oval from the center of 1 index card.

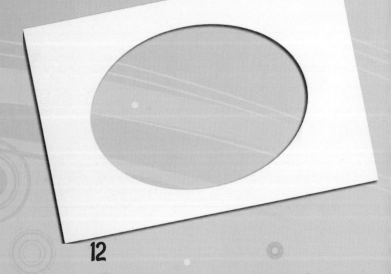

12

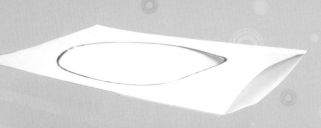

2. On the other index card, glue along 3 sides, leaving one short side without glue. Place the cut index card lines-side-down onto the glue and let dry. A picture can slide into the frame through the side that has not been glued.

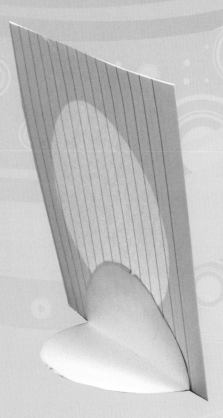

3. To make a stand for the frame, fold the oval that you cut from the index card in half. Glue it to the back of the picture frame at the bottom of the frame. Unfold the oval.

4. Decorate the frame by gluing paper knots on the front. Curl the tails of the paper knots, or let them hang down. Add a favorite photo.

PAPER CUTTING FROM CHINA

The Chinese invented paper. Paper cutting is a Chinese art form, and the fancy paper cuts are used to decorate windows, lamps, doors, and gifts.

A traditional paper cut decorates a wall.

WHAT YOU WILL NEED

- pencil
- white and colored paper
- scissors
- glitter (optional)
- glue (optional)
- markers (optional)

---

1. Make a paper cut pattern on white paper. You can use any shape you'd like, or you can follow the pattern on page 27.

2. Trace onto colored paper. Cut out the shape. Carefully cut out all the black shapes inside the paper cutting.

3. Decorate with markers, glitter, or anything you wish. Use the paper cuts to decorate notebooks, binders, windows, or doors.

THEATER MASK FROM INDONESIA

Outdoor theater is a common form of entertainment in Indonesia. The actors in these plays wear masks. Some masks are symbols for gods or characters. Others show characters' emotions. Make up a play and create masks to go with it.

Balinese masks help create characters and serve as decorations.

WHAT YOU WILL NEED

- scissors
- paper plate
- paintbrush
- craft stick
- puff paint, poster paint, or markers (optional)
- glitter and feathers
- craft stick

1. Cut out eyes and a mouth from the paper plate.

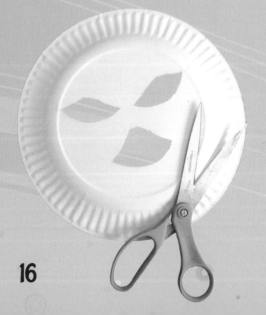

2. Decorate the mask using puff paint, poster paint, markers, or even glitter and feathers. Let dry.

3. Glue the craft stick to the bottom of the mask and let dry.

4. Use the mask in a play or hang on the wall.

17

TIBETAN SAND MANDALA

Mandala *means "circle" in the Sanskrit language. Tibetan monks use sand and paint to make colorful circle designs called mandalas. These mandalas are part of the Buddhist religion, as well as pieces of art.*

This Buddhist monk is creating a sand mandala.

WHAT YOU WILL NEED

- scissors
- poster board or paper plate
- pencil
- ruler
- glue
- paintbrush
- colored sand or glitter
- clear contact paper

1. Cut a circle from a piece of poster board. Or simply use a paper plate. Copy the sand mandala pattern from page 28 onto the circle. Or you could make up your own design with a ruler. Decide what color each piece of the design will be. Lightly write, in pencil, that color in the design.

2. Pour glue onto the paper circle. Use a paintbrush to brush glue onto a part of the design. Then, pour the right color of sand or glitter onto that part of the design. Let dry, then pour the extra sand or glitter back into the container. Continue with this until the design is finished.

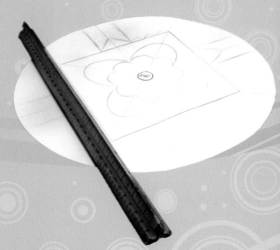

3. Let the mandala dry overnight. Display on a table or counter. If hanging on a wall, cover the mandala with clear contact paper to keep the sand or glitter from falling off.

EMAKI STORY SCROLL

Emaki *are Japanese scrolls that are read as they are unrolled. They tell stories and often have illustrations.*

This emaki is from the sixteenth century.

WHAT YOU WILL NEED

◉ **clear tape**

◉ **construction paper**

◉ **glue**

◉ **2 unsharpened pencils**

◉ **paint, markers, or crayons**

1. Tape 5 pieces of construction paper together to make 1 banner.

2. Make a line of glue along the top and bottom edges of the banner. Press the pencils to the line of glue and let dry.

3. Use paint, markers, or crayons to write a story and draw pictures on the banner.

4. Roll the pencil on the right so the paper wraps around it. Keep rolling until reaching the pencil on the left.

5. Unroll the paper to read the story. Roll up again to carry or put it away.

ORIGAMI JUMPING FROG

Origami means "to fold paper" in Japanese. But you can use scissors, glue, or tape to create flowers, animals, people, or anything else you can think of.

This young boy is creating origami.

1. Fold half a piece of construction paper diagonally to make a triangle. Unfold.

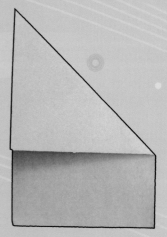

2. Fold the paper on the other diagonal to make a triangle. Unfold. There should be an X on the top part of the paper.

22

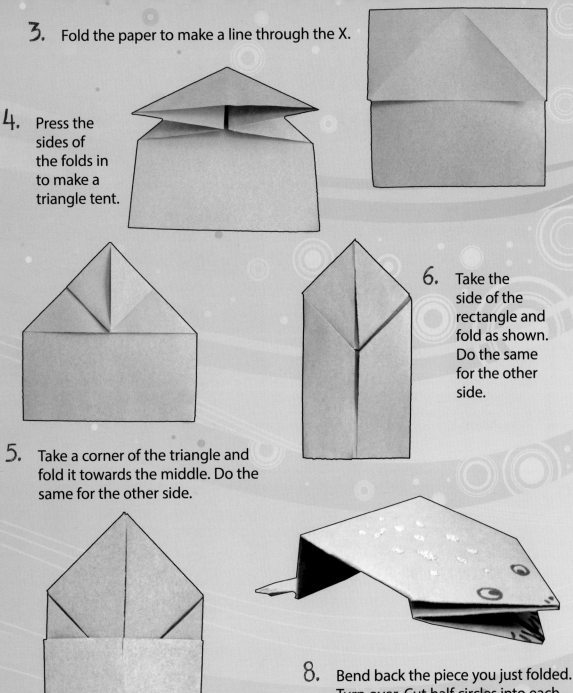

3. Fold the paper to make a line through the X.

4. Press the sides of the folds in to make a triangle tent.

5. Take a corner of the triangle and fold it towards the middle. Do the same for the other side.

6. Take the side of the rectangle and fold as shown. Do the same for the other side.

7. Fold the bottom in half to the top.

8. Bend back the piece you just folded. Turn over. Cut half circles into each back leg. Make a "U" shape between the legs to give them shape. Decorate the frog with markers and glitter. Your frog is ready to hop!

23

Paper Non From Vietnam

In Vietnam, a non is a cone-shaped hat. Make a non to wear to keep you cool on sunny days.

Vietnamese people wear nons to keep the sun off their faces.

What You Will Need

- 🌀 large white poster board
- 🌀 scissors
- 🌀 glue
- 🌀 hole punch
- 🌀 markers, paint, glitter, or crayons
- 🌀 yarn

1. Cut out a large circle from a piece of poster board.

24

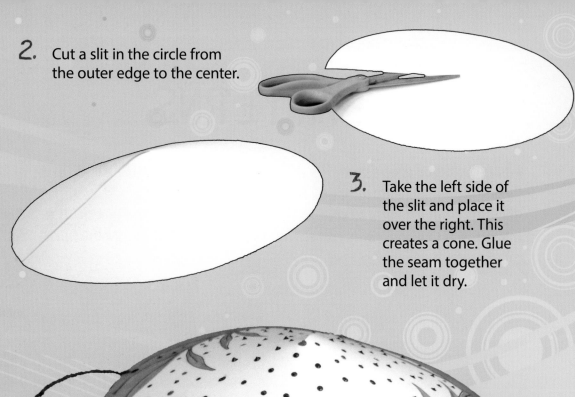

2. Cut a slit in the circle from the outer edge to the center.

3. Take the left side of the slit and place it over the right. This creates a cone. Glue the seam together and let it dry.

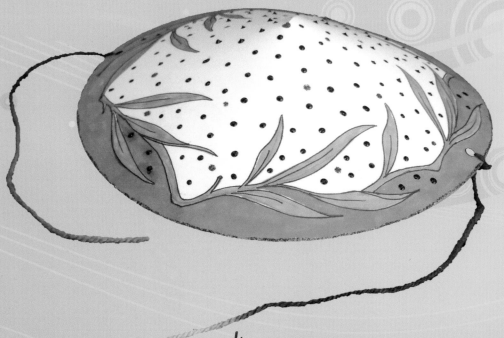

4. Decorate the cone with markers, paint, glitter, or crayons. Punch holes in opposite edges of the cone and tie a piece of yarn from one hole to the other. This will keep the hat from falling off your head.

PATTERNS

The percentages included on the patterns tell you how much to enlarge or shrink the image using a copier. Most copiers and printers have an adjustable size/percentage feature to change the size of an image when you print it. After you print the pattern to its correct size, cut it out. Trace it onto the material listed in the craft.

At 100%

Knot Frame

Butterfly Paper Cut Out

At 100%

Mandala

Enlarge by 165%

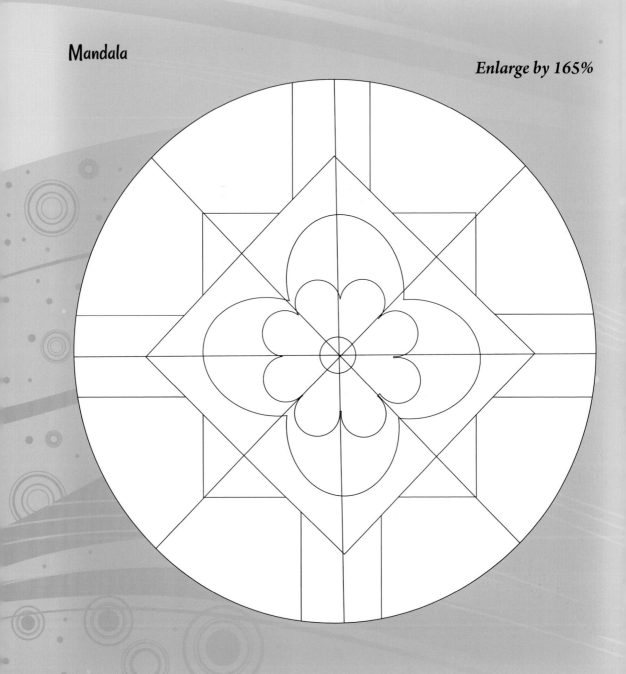

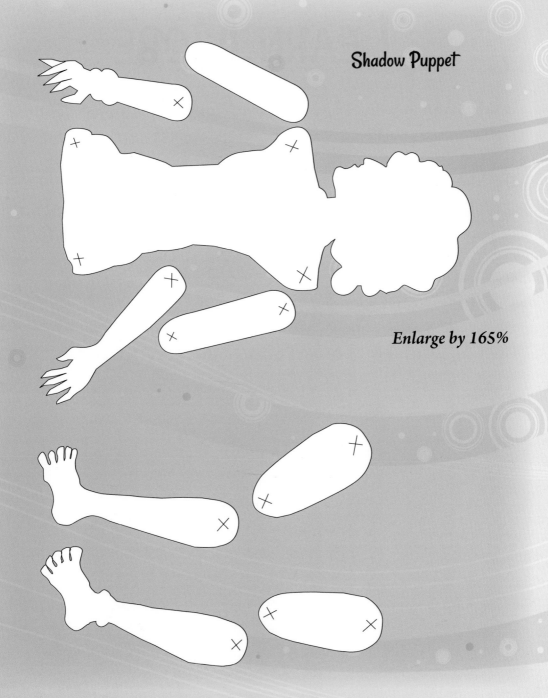

Shadow Puppet

Enlarge by 165%

29

Learn More

Bowler, Ann Martin. *All About Korea*. North Clarendon, Vt.: Tuttle Publishing, 2011.

DeCristoforo, Jennifer. *Lucky Bamboo Book of Crafts: Over 100 Projects and Ideas Celebrating Chinese Culture*. Yarmouth, Maine: Jennifer DeCristoforo, 2013.

Heapy, Teresa. *Japanese Culture*. Portsmouth, N.H.: Heinemann, 2012.

Guillain, Charlotte. *Vietnam*. Portsmouth, N.H.: Heinemann, 2012.

WEB SITES

freekidscrafts.com/world-crafts/asian-crafts/

More Asian crafts!

pbslearningmedia.org/resource/arct14.arts.zjaegi/jaegi/

Learn how to make a jaegi, a toy from Korea.

teacher.scholastic.com/activities/asian-american/print.htm

More activities that explore Asian cultures.

INDEX

B
Bali, 10
brass fasteners, 10–11

C
China, 4–5, 14
clear contact paper, 18–19
clear tape, 10, 20
colored
    paper, 12, 14–15
    sand, 18–19
construction paper, 5–7, 20, 22
craft stick, 8–9, 16–17
crayons, 6–7, 20–21, 24–25

D
drinking straw, 10

E
emaki, 20

G
glitter, 14–19, 22–24
glue, 6, 8–9, 12–14, 17–22, 24–25

H
hole punch, 10, 24–25

I
index cards, 6, 12
Indonesia, 4, 16

J
Japan, 6, 8, 22
Japanese
    fans, 8
    scrolls, 20–21
    storytellers, 6

K
knots, 12–13
Korea, 12

L
lanterns, 5

M
mandala, 18–19, 28
markers, 6–8, 14–16, 20–25
masks, 5, 16–17

N
non, 24

O
origami, 22

P
paint, 18, 20–21, 24–25
paintbrush, 16, 18–19
paper, 7–8, 12–14, 21–22, 24, 27
    cutting, 5, 14–15
    plate, 8, 16, 18
patterns, 26–29
pencil, 10, 12, 14, 18, 20–21

poster
    board, 8, 10, 18, 24
    paint, 16
puff paint, 16–17
puppets, 10–11

R
ruler, 18

S
Sanskrit, 18
scissors, 6, 8, 10, 12, 14, 16, 22, 24
shadow plays, 10
shoebox, 5–6

T
tape, 10–11, 20, 22
Tibetan, 18

U
unsharpened pencil, 20

V
Vietnam, 24

Y
yarn, 24–25

Z
Zen, 5